AF488081

Some Starseeds have lived on many different planets. Most Starseeds are very old, wise souls. Some star races have chosen to help Earth become a better place and they help us in different ways from space or by connecting to our soul.

Let's take a journey through space to visit some of our star family. They can visit us in dream time, meditation and anytime we ask to connect. Some star beings can come through a portal or with a spaceship to visit Earth.

Starseeds are souls from other star systems who came to live on Earth to help create a new Earth. In the new Earth love and freedom will be most important. Humans and Extraterrestrials will live in peace and harmony with Mother Earth and with all living beings.

Starseeds have a deep love for Mother Nature, love to explore the Earth and love looking at the Sky. Starseeds have a passion to make the world a better place and want to help others. Starseeds all have different missions to help humanity evolve.

Some Starseeds feel homesick. Your star family wants to remind you to enjoy all the beauty Mother Earth has to offer. They will welcome you back when your mission on Earth is completed.

Your star family is always with you. They are guiding you on your mission to heal the Earth. Just close your eyes and ask to connect. You will feel their love and can hear their messages when your mind is calm and quiet.

You may remember Languages of Light that can help you heal and give strength for your journey. Light Languages are from your lifetimes as star beings and can help you remember where you came from. Messages are sent to your soul through light codes and can be felt with your heart.

We are the Andromedans from the Andromeda Galaxy. Even though our skin is different colors we are all the same. We love freedom and want freedom for all humans and animals on Earth. Our ships monitor the skies and sometimes cleanse your air.

We are the Antareans and are gateway keepers of the Higher Realms. We are protectors of the galaxy and the keepers of the Antares Stargate. Many souls choose to pass through the Antares gateway to reactivate soul memory before incarnating in the physical realm.

We live on Sirius B, a planet from the Sirius Star System that is covered with beautiful blue water. The dolphins sing tunes that cleanse and heal everyone in our oceans. We have sent some of our dolphins to do the same for your oceans. We send out vibrations of love and peace to Earth.

Lyrans are the Cosmic ancestors of all humans in our Galaxy. We are the Lyran Avians. We learn fast and easily. We learned to teleport and evolved into higher dimensions. Most of us are scientists, explorers and philosophers. We are mammals even though we have some bird features. We had many different races on our planet who lived in harmony and peace.

We are the Lyran Felines from the Lyra Star System and are humanoids. We are some of the oldest souls in the galaxy. We are very wise, peaceful and united in love. We came to live in Atlantis on Earth and other planets when our home was destroyed in the Lyra-Draco war by another race who wanted to take over our planet and use us as slaves.

We are the Pleiadians from Pleiades, a beautiful star cluster known as the Seven Sisters. We love meditating, yoga, crystals, nature and taking care of our planet. We love to do energy healing such as Reiki. We look very similar to humans.

We are the Blue Avians and we exist in the higher dimensions. Our spaceships look like balls and are in your skies around Earth. We help humans to evolve. The birds on Earth are a gift from us to help regulate the electromagnetic atmosphere. Birds sing light codes that bring healing to everyone who hears their songs.

We are the Arcturians and we heal with energy and crystals. We send healing light to everyone on Earth and assist in healing for humans when they ask us for help. We are spiritual guardians of the galaxy. We love music.

We are the Lemurians and were the first galactic star beings to step foot on Mother Earth. We are the keepers of Mother Earth as Shamans and Healers. Our mission is to care for the land and resources. Mother Earth is a living breathing being who is loved, respected and honored.

We are part of the Galactic
Federation. Our group of
Cosmic Beings come from
many star systems. We help
Earth and other planets become
more loving and peaceful. We
want all beings to live in unity
in the Divine and to remember
that you are loved.

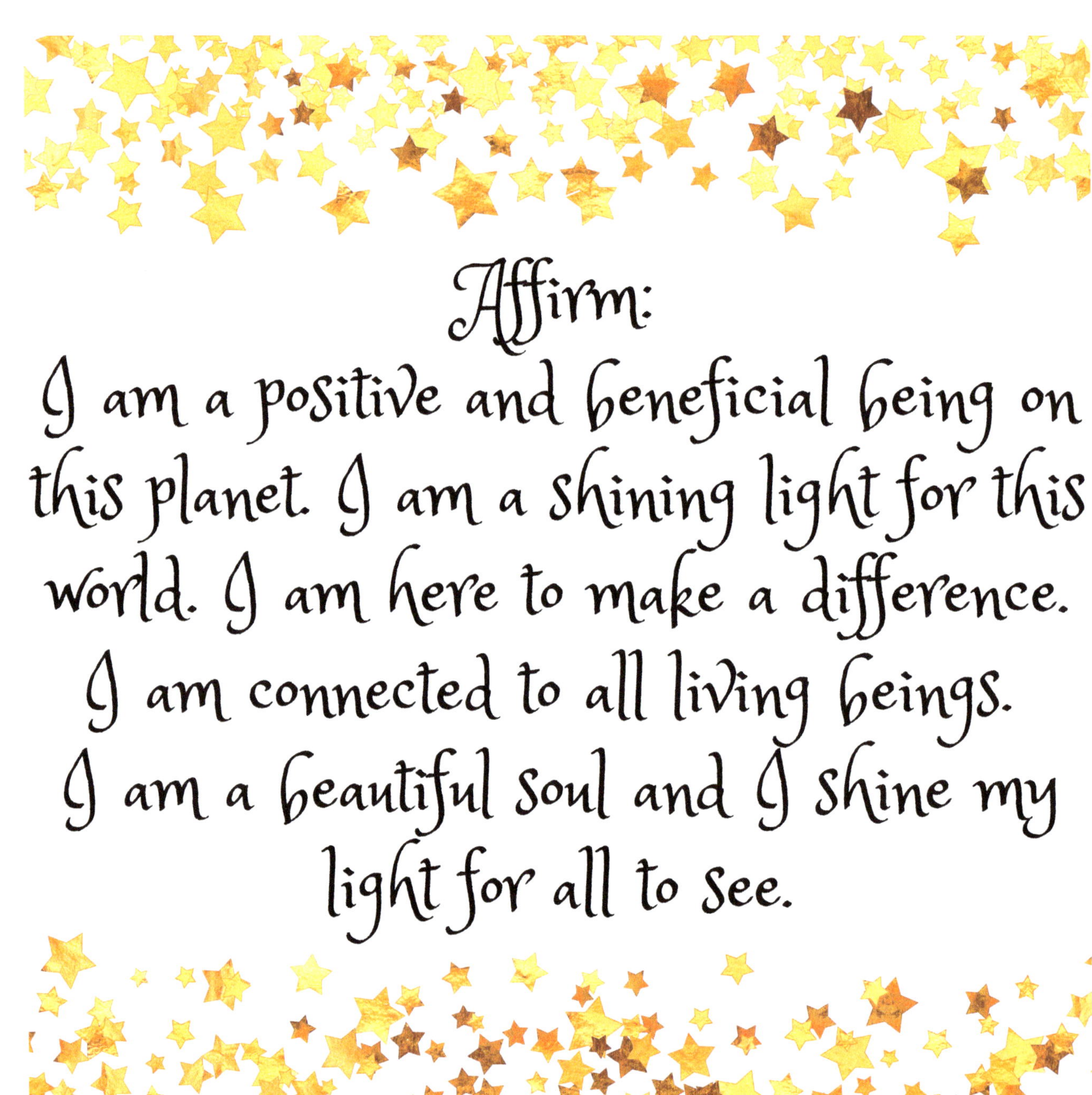

Affirm:
I am a positive and beneficial being on this planet. I am a shining light for this world. I am here to make a difference. I am connected to all living beings. I am a beautiful soul and I shine my light for all to see.

Dedicated to my SiSTAR
Sunshiiine & Kugel I ♥ U

Dedicated to my SiSTAR
Sunshiiine & Kugel I ♥ U